AMAZING PLANT POWERS

How Plants Fly, Fight, Hide, Hunt, & Change the World

Loreen Leedy & Andrew Schuerger

Holiday House · New York

Let's look at some common **plant parts**.

Not all plants have every part.

bud

flower

leaf

stem

seed

sprout

roots

bulb

roots

Every plant needs **light**, **water**, **air**, and **minerals** to live.

I don't have a bulb.

I do! I do!

Calcium is a mineral, right?

CARBON DIOXIDE

LIGHT

Let's start with the **most important** plant power of all.

Green chlorophyll

PHOTOSYNTHESIS =

What is it?

Pretty flowers?

OXYGEN

All plants use **light** to **make food** for themselves. Along the way they release **oxygen**, which people and animals need to breathe.

This process is called **photosynthesis**.

absorbs sunlight.

A Plant Food Factory

SUGARS
to feed the plant

WOW! What else can plants do?!?

WATER and MINERALS from roots

Plants need  **water,** and some can even live in it!

Do you mean in a boat?

water lilies

cypress trees

Floating stems let water lily leaves stay on the surface.

knees

wide trunk

Plant roots hold soil, which reduces erosion and preserves clean water.

Wide trunks and **"knees"** keep cypress trees standing tall in soggy soil.

These aquatic plants have **flexible stems** that bend with the force of ocean waves.

It's too wet for me!

surfgrass at low tide

Mangroves have stilts!

mangrove prop root

Prop roots
ve a good grip in wet ground.

Salt-filtering roots
allow mangroves to live in seawater.

 **Dry** places and seasons are tough to survive.

barrel cactus

Many cacti have **no leaves,** which reduces water loss.

It's too dry for me!

Ponytail palms are also called "elephant's foot" because of their bulbous base.

Thick trunks, leaves, or **stems** can store water during dry times.

The thick, colorful leaves of these succulent plants resemble flower petals.

8

Those ferns look dead.

Some plants can **wilt** when it's dry, then **revive** when it rains again.

Yippee...they turned green again!

resurrection fern

Many plants have **long roots** to reach water deep underground.

switchgrass

Wildflowers with a **fast life cycle** quickly bloom and make seeds after rain falls.

California poppies and other wildflowers

9

Shade

makes it hard for plants to get enough light.

Will a flashlight help?

Vines **climb up** trees or objects to reach the sunlight.

oak tree

philodendron

That vine is my cousin!

Plants can **bend** toward light.

Large, dark leaves can absorb more light.

alocasia

Some flowering plants **sprout early in spring** before the trees grow new leaves.

trillium

I don't like this gloomy shade.

Growing taller allows plants to get more light.

Redwoods are the tallest trees on Earth.

11

What can plants do about **cold**

Many trees stop growing and **drop their leaves** in winter.

maple leaves

"Antifreeze" sap in conifer needles prevents freezing.

conifer tree

In the arctic, plants grow **close to the ground** to stay out of icy winds.

arctic plants

heat?

Help, we're wilting!

Sunlight hits pad's edge.

Vertical cactus pads avoid the sun's hottest rays.

prickly pear cactus

Some plants have pale colors such as gray to **reflect the sun's heat.**

Small, fuzzy leaves block heat and retain water.

This cactus has so **many spines,** they create shade for the stems.

sagebrush

teddy bear cholla

13

Plants can't run from  **fire!**

Thick bark protected this tree from the flames.

Seeds that are **released by heat** will sprout after the fire.

lodgepole pinecone

It's still alive!

Tough plants can **grow again** after being burned.

pine

palmetto

14

 can damage plants.

Trees that are **cone shaped** can shed heavy snow.

palm

Flexible stems and **leaves** won't break in strong winds.

This weather is awful!

Oh nooooo!

fir

Some plants can **lerate flooding** after heavy rains.

red maple and other trees

Soils

may not be ideal for plant growth.

Loose sand can be held together by **long roots**.

Carnivorous plants live in poor soil, so they **hunt insects** for extra nutrients.

sunde

Venus flytrap

What do flies taste like?

root nodule

The sundew traps bugs with sticky drops!

Soil bacteria in root nodules help peas and beans **make fertilizer**.

Some plants need **no soil** at all!

Air plants **grow on other plants.**

Air plants hold on with their roots but don't hurt their hosts.

Lichens are teams of algae and fungi.

Lichens can **grow on bare rock.**

I like my roots in the dirt.

After volcanoes erupt, tough **pioneer plants** sprout in the cooled lava.

ferns

New plants grow in many ways!

aspens

I started out as a cutting.

← spore case

Dust-sized **spores** will become new ferns.

All these trees grew out of the **same root system.**

kalanchoe

Tiny plantlets have formed on this **leaf edge**.

new sprout →

An old **stem** can take root and start a new plant.

The **leafy top** of an old pineapple can produce a new fruit.

18

pineapple

Pollinators help flowers make  **seeds!**

Pollen is usually yellow.

bee on a lantana flower

Flowers use **color, scent,** or **nectar** to attract bees and other pollinators.

Monarch butterfly on a buddleia flower

Seeds come in many **sizes** and **shapes**.

pumpkin

various garden seeds

sweet gum seed pod

grass seed head

Indian corn

Seeds **travel** in a variety of ways.

Some can **fly** in the breeze.

maple

Some seeds **hitchhike** on fur or clothing.

They hang on with tiny hooks!

dandelion

garberia

Coconuts **float** many miles on ocean currents.

Dandelion seeds float like tiny parachutes.

Coconut palms grow in the tropics.

Tasty fruit

attracts hungry animals that spit out the seeds or pass them in droppings.

blueberries

strawberry

Are those sausages?

ild bananas have large seeds.

banana

Squirrels and many other animals **store seeds,** which can sprout if not eaten.

Giraffes like to eat the fruit of sausage trees.

Do giraffes eat daisies?

Hungry bugs can hurt or even kill a plant.

Insects may eat any part, including leaves, flowers, stems, roots, and seeds.

Bugs are scary!

leafcutter ant

bean

Somebody, please help!

aphids

Yummy!

Beneficial insects such as ladybugs eat plant pests.

Aphids suck plant fluids.

grasshoppers feeding on wheat

Confederate jasmine ~as latex, a milky fluid that deters pests.

latex

Plants can often **outgrow** insect damage.

Geranium petals temporarily paralyze Japanese beetles.

Many plants use **toxins** to defend themselves.

Insects are repelled by a **strong** or **bitter** smell or taste.

Eucalyptus tree leaves contain a pungent oil.

Many bugs don't like to eat mint.

spearmint

23

Hungry animals

are a constant threat.

A green, unripe orange tastes sour.

A **bad flavor** can discourage nibbling.

holly

Many plants fight back with **spines** or **thorns**.

???

acacia tree

silk floss tree

pebble plant

Pebble plants **hide** by looking like stones.

When these leaves are touched,
they **fold up** and seem to vanish.

What a neat trick!

sensitive plant

Toxic plants may cause discomfort, vomiting, or even death when touched or eaten.

Grass can **regrow** quickly after being grazed.

grass

Many familiar plants such as azaleas are poisonous.

Grapes, raisins, onions, and other "people food" can make dogs and other pets sick.

I had no idea!

Dieffenbachia and other houseplants can make pets ill.

25

People need plants!

People eat **fruits, vegetables, nuts, grains,** and other plant products.

cotton

People wear clothing made from **plant fibers** such as cotton

People use **wood** from trees to make buildings, paper, furniture, musical instruments, boats, and many other things.

26

People need us!

A person planted me.

People grow plants in **pots** and **orchards** and **gardens** and **fields** and anywhere else plants can live.

vegetable garden

a grove of orange trees

That hairstyle is un-be-LEAF-able!

cornfield

27

Without plants,
the land would
be nothing but
bare rocks and **dirt**!

Plants have the power
to make **forests**
and **farms**
and **parks**
and **prairies**
and **meadows**
and **marshes**
and much more.

That's so true!

They provide **shade, fresh air,** and **clean water.**

They **feed** and **shelter** the whole world!

So the next time you see a plant, why not say **"Thank you"**?

Hooray for plants!

We do have AMAZING powers!

29

Plant projects

Plant Power Scavenger Hunt

Visit a garden and see how many plant powers you can spot. Make notes in a journal, draw sketches, and take photographs.

My Plant Power

Imagine a plant power you could have, then write a story. What would be good and bad about having the power?

Plants for Lunch

Look at the fruits and vegetables on the lunch menu. What plant parts could you choose? Are there flower buds (broccoli), stems (celery), bulbs (onions), seeds (peas), roots (carrots), or fruits (cherries)?

Kitchen Scrap Garden

Grow new plants with recycled fruits and vegetables such as lemon seeds, pineapple tops, cut-up potatoes, and avocado seeds.

Glossary

algae	a group of simple, nonflowering plants; green algae are the ancestors of all plants
bulb	a rounded underground storage organ found in plants such as onions
chlorophyll	the green pigment that absorbs light for photosynthesis
flower	the seed-producing part of a plant
photosynthesis	the plant process of using sunlight, carbon dioxide, minerals, and water to make sugars and release oxygen
pollen	the yellow, powdery substance used by flowers in making seeds
roots	the parts that anchor plants (usually in soil) and absorb water and minerals
seed	the structure a flowering plant makes to reproduce itself
spore	a dust-like particle that a simple nonflowering plant makes to reproduce itself
stem	the main stalk of a plant
toxic	poisonous
trunk	the main woody stem of a tree

Algae have chlorophyll but do not have true roots, stems, or leaves.

Land plants produce a large portion of the oxygen on Earth. The rest is made by one-celled phytoplankton that live in the ocean.

Lichens are not true plants because they are teams of algae and fungi.

Find activities and resources for this book at www.LoreenLeedy.com.

Did you know there's an animal that
has plants living on it?
This mammal lives in trees and
moves very, very slowly. . . .

Text copyright © 2015 by Loreen Leedy and Andrew Schuerger
Illustrations copyright © 2015 by Loreen Leedy
Photographs, except those listed on page 30, copyright © 2015 by Andrew Schuerger
All Rights Reserved
HOLIDAY HOUSE is registered in the U.S. Patent and Trademark Office.
Printed and Bound in October 2014 at Toppan Leefung, DongGuan City, China..
The artwork was created digitally.
www.holidayhouse.com
First Edition
1 3 5 7 9 10 8 6 4 2

Library of Congress Cataloging-in-Publication Data
Leedy, Loreen, author, illustrator.
Amazing plant powers : how plants fly, fight, hide, hunt, and change the world /
by Loreen Leedy and Andrew Schuerger. — First edition.
pages cm
ISBN 978-0-8234-2256-2 (hardcover)
1. Plants—Juvenile literature. I. Schuerger, Andrew, author. II. Title.
QK49.L45 2015
580—dc23
2014028430

To our photosynthesizing friends on Earth—L.L.

I want to live on a giraffe

It's a sloth! Sloths have
a greenish color because
algae grows
on their hair.